POLAR
EXPLORATION
JOURNEYS TO THE ARCTIC AND ANTARCTIC

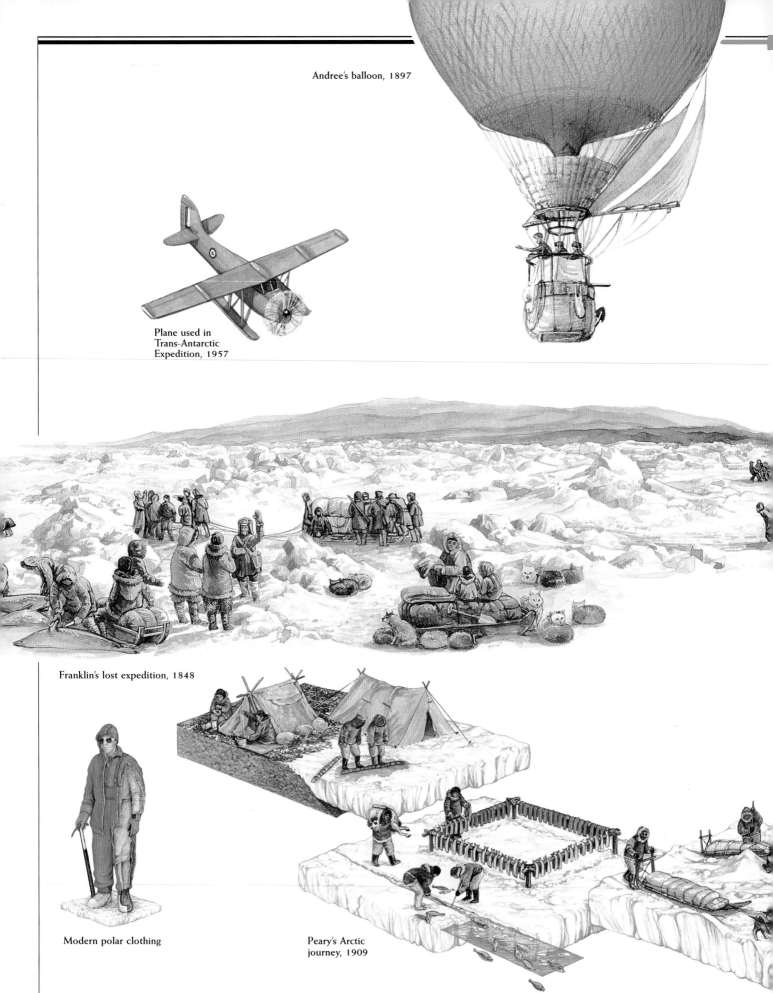

Andrée's balloon, 1897

Plane used in
Trans-Antarctic
Expedition, 1957

Franklin's lost expedition, 1848

Modern polar clothing

Peary's Arctic
journey, 1909

POLAR
EXPLORATION
JOURNEYS TO THE ARCTIC AND ANTARCTIC

Written by
MARTYN BRAMWELL

Illustrated by
MARJE CROSBY-FAIRALL
and ANN WINTERBOTHAM

DK PUBLISHING, INC.

A DK PUBLISHING BOOK

Project Editor Emma Johnson
Design and Visualization James Marks
Senior Art Editor Vicky Wharton
Senior Editor Scarlett O'Hara
Senior Managing Editor Linda Martin
Senior Managing Art Editor Julia Harris
DTP Designer Almudena Díaz
Picture Research Catherine Edkins
Jacket Designer Mark Haygarth
Production Lisa Moss
Consultant Bernard Stonehouse
US Editor William Lach

First American Edition, 1998
4 6 8 10 9 7 5 3

Published in the United States by
DK Publishing, Inc.
95 Madison Avenue, New York, New York 10016

Copyright © 1998 Dorling Kindersley Ltd., London

Visit us on the World Wide Web at
http://www.dk.com

Published in Great Britain by Dorling Kindersley Limited.

Library of Congress Cataloging-in-Publication Data

Bramwell, Martyn.
 Polar exploration: journeys to the Arctic and Antarctic / written by Martyn
  Bramwell. – 1st American ed.
 p.   cm. -- (DK discoveries)
 Summary: Describes some of the many explorations made to both the North
 and South Poles.
 ISBN 0-7894-3421-0 (alk. paper)
 1. Explorers--Great Britain--Biography--Juvenile liternature.
 2. Explorers--United States--Biography--Juvenile literature.
 3. Polar regions--Discovery and exploration--Juvenile literature.
 [1. Explorers. 2. Polar regions--Discovery and exploration.]
 I. Title. II. Series.   98-4221
 G584.B7 1998   CIP
 919.804--dc21   AC

Reproduced by Colourscan, Singapore
Printed and bound by L.E.G.O., Italy

Contents

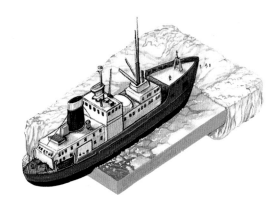

First
Encounters

A T THE TWO ENDS of the Earth lie the Arctic and the
Antarctic. Into these icy worlds came sealers and whalers
looking for new hunting grounds, explorers searching for new
trade routes, and scientists and seamen on
voyages of discovery.

A ship of the Franklin search
fleet, August 20, 1851

On sailing ships, masts and rigging could become so encrusted with frozen sea spray that the ship could become top-heavy and capsize.

"About seven the edge of the ice took the ship under the lee gangway, shaking her throughout. Yielding inch by inch before such a powerful lever, the ship at length rested on her keel, but it was but momentary, for in a second she was thrown over on her side..."

George McDougall,
Sailing Master of the *Resolute*,
a ship of the Franklin search fleet, 1852

Jumbled ridges of sea ice can rise higher than a ship's deck.

INTO THE ARCTIC OCEAN

IT WAS NOT UNTIL THE SIXTEENTH century that European seafarers ventured into the Arctic Ocean. They wanted to find a short route to the riches of China and the Spice Islands of the East Indies. If they could cut across the top of North America (the Northwest Passage) or Asia (the Northeast Passage), they could shorten the journey to China by months. There wcre many attempts to find a Northwest Passage (see pages 14–15), but it was the Norwegian explorer Roald Amundsen who first found a way in 1905. The first complete journey through the Northeast Passage was made by Adolf Erik Nordenskiöld in his ship *Vega* in 1878–9. These voyages paved the way for later attempts to reach the North Pole.

SET ADRIFT

In 1610 Henry Hudson discovered Hudson Bay on his ship *Discovery*. Having failed to find a Northwest Passage he was forced to winter there. He died when his crew mutinied and set him adrift in a small boat with his son and a few loyal crewmen.

ESKIMO COUPLE

In 1576, when Sir Martin Frobisher sailed as far north as Baffin Island, he encountered the Inuit (Eskimo) people of the Arctic. In one account he described their "hose," or leggings: "In cold weather or winter, they wear the fur side inward; and in summer outward." This Inuit man and woman were captured by Frobisher and taken back to England, where they died.

EARLY VOYAGES IN ARCTIC WATERS	
Martin Frobisher	1576–8
John Davis	1586–7
Willem Barents	1596
Henry Hudson	1610
Vitus Bering	1733–6
John Ross	1818
William E. Parry	1819–20

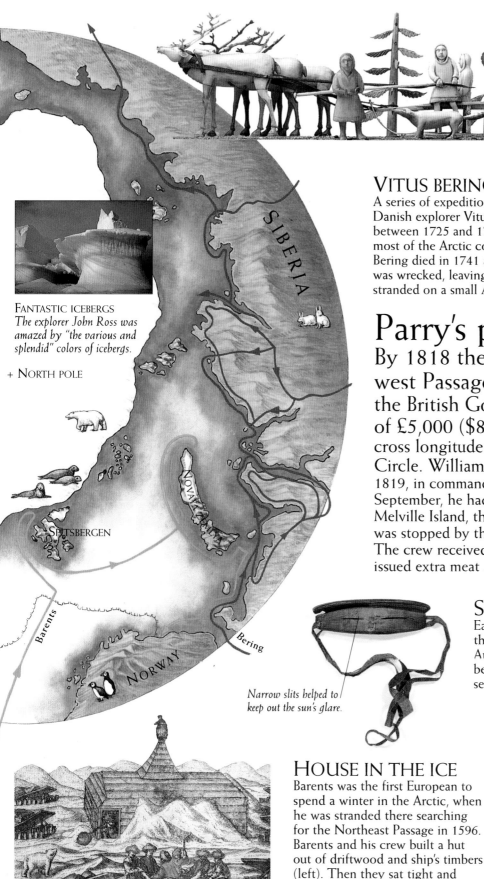

REINDEER HUNTERS

As well as pulling sleds, reindeer provided food, clothing, tools, and material for tents for the Siberian reindeer hunters of the Arctic – the Chukchi, the Samoyed, and the Yakut.

FANTASTIC ICEBERGS
The explorer John Ross was amazed by "the various and splendid" colors of icebergs.

+ NORTH POLE

SIBERIA

NOVAYA ZEMLYA

SPITSBERGEN

Barents

Bering

NORWAY

VITUS BERING

A series of expeditions led by the Danish explorer Vitus Bering between 1725 and 1743 mapped most of the Arctic coast of Asia. Bering died in 1741 after his ship was wrecked, leaving him stranded on a small Arctic island.

Parry's prize

By 1818 the search for a Northwest Passage was heating up, and the British Government offered a prize of £5,000 ($8,000) to the first ship to cross longitude 110°W inside the Arctic Circle. William Edward Parry set off in May 1819, in command of the ships *Hecla* and *Griper*. By September, he had pushed through the ice as far as Melville Island, the farthest west so far. At 112°W he was stopped by thick ice, but he had won the prize. The crew received a share of the money, and Parry issued extra meat and beer for Sunday dinner.

SNOW GOGGLES

Early explorers wore goggles to protect their eyes from the intense glare of the Arctic sun. These snow goggles (left) belonged to William Parry, who went in search of the Northwest Passage in 1819.

Narrow slits helped to keep out the sun's glare.

HOUSE IN THE ICE

Barents was the first European to spend a winter in the Arctic, when he was stranded there searching for the Northeast Passage in 1596. Barents and his crew built a hut out of driftwood and ship's timbers (left). Then they sat tight and waited for the ice to thaw so that they could set sail for home.

FACT file

- The Arctic Ocean covers an area of about 5,440,000 sq miles (14,090,000 sq km).

- The Arctic Ocean surface water averages 30°F (–1°C) in summer and 28°F (–2°C) in winter.

- The Arctic's greatest depth is more than 13,000 ft (4,000 m). It averages 4,360 ft (1,300 m) deep.

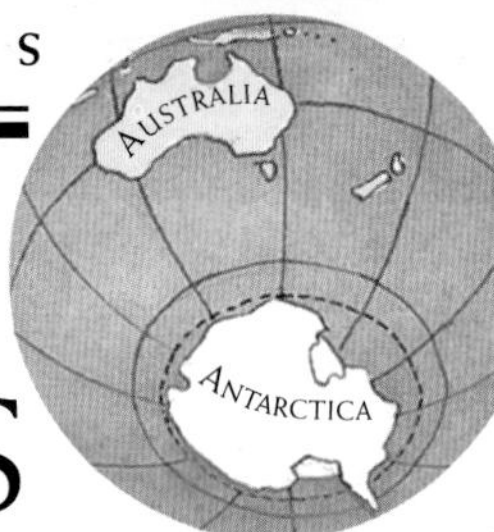

SOUTHBOUND SCIENTISTS AND SEALERS

LONG BEFORE ANYONE SAW ANTARCTICA, scientists in many countries believed that a huge southern continent existed. They called it *terra australis incognita* (the unknown southern land). Captain James Cook, the great 18th-century explorer, was the first to cross the Antarctic Circle. Over the next 100 years the coastline of Antarctica was mapped by the sealers, whalers, explorers, and scientists who followed Russian Admiral von Bellingshausen, American Nathaniel Palmer, and English naval officer Edward Bransfield all reported sighting the Antarctic Peninsula in 1820, but whether they saw the mainland or one of the islands is not known. They were followed by Charles Wilkes, Dumont d'Urville, James Clark Ross, and others. In 1898, Norwegian explorer Carsten Borchgrevink led the first party to spend a whole winter in Antarctica – setting the scene for the heroic age of exploration.

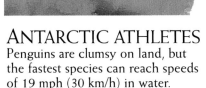

ANTARCTIC ATHLETES

Penguins are clumsy on land, but the fastest species can reach speeds of 19 mph (30 km/h) in water.

TIME TO RELAX

The American naval officer Charles Wilkes mapped the coastal area of Antarctica now called Wilkes Land. In 1840 his crew landed on an iceberg to collect water and had fun sliding down it.

BASKING SEALS

Antarctic seals spend hours sunbathing on ice floes. The crabeater seal is one of six Antarctic species.

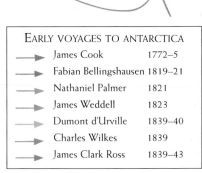

EARLY VOYAGES TO ANTARCTICA

James Cook	1772–5
Fabian Bellingshausen	1819–21
Nathaniel Palmer	1821
James Weddell	1823
Dumont d'Urville	1839–40
Charles Wilkes	1839
James Clark Ross	1839–43

NAVIGATOR'S WATCH

Navigators used special watches called chronometers to calculate their position at sea. This one (right) belonged to Captain Cook.

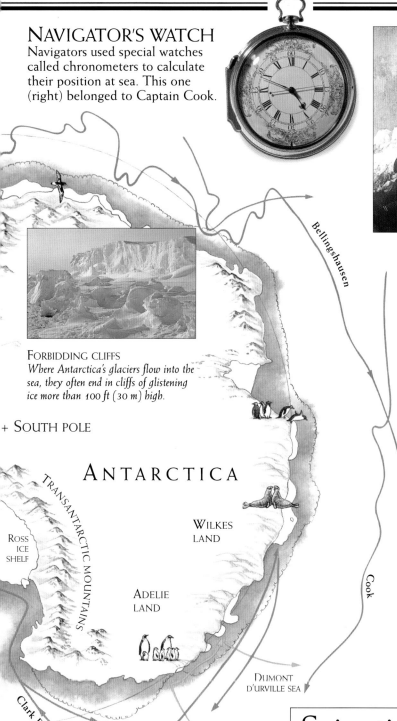

FORBIDDING CLIFFS
Where Antarctica's glaciers flow into the sea, they often end in cliffs of glistening ice more than 100 ft (30 m) high.

+ SOUTH POLE

ANTARCTICA

TRANSANTARCTIC MOUNTAINS

ROSS ICE SHELF

WILKES LAND

ADELIE LAND

DUMONT D'URVILLE SEA

Bellingshausen

Cook

Clark Ross

Wilkes

d'Urville

CAPTAIN COOK GOES SOUTH

In 1772, Cook's orders from the British Admiralty were to try and find the "southern land," study its rocks, animals, and plants, and make friends with the native people, if there were any. Cook did not find Antarctica, but his reports of the rich sea life of the unexplored Southern Ocean attracted hundreds of sealers and whalers to the area.

IN STORMY SEAS

Frenchman Dumont d'Urville charted part of the Antarctic Peninsula in 1837, in the ships *Astrolabe* and *Zelée*. In 1840 he returned, this time to the opposite side of the continent, where he named *Terre Adélie* (Adelie Land) after his wife Adéle.

Scientist on board

JOSEPH DALTON HOOKER, who later became Director of the Royal Botanic Gardens at Kew, England, was a young man when he traveled south with Sir James Clark Ross. Hooker went on several expeditions in search of botanical specimens.

Anisotome latifolia

A botanical drawing from one of Hooker's Antarctic voyages.

FACT file

• Antarctica is almost twice the size of Australia. The continent covers 5,500,000 sq miles (14,245,000 sq km).

• If the ice in Antarctica melted, the world's sea level would rise 200 ft (60 m).

• The Ross Ice Shelf is as big as the state of Texas.

South
Through the Ross Sea

BRITISH NAVAL OFFICER JAMES CLARK ROSS WAS MORE THAN just a brilliant navigator. He was also a scientist, with a keen interest in the Earth's magnetic field. In 1831, during an Arctic voyage with his uncle Sir John Ross, he had located the North Magnetic Pole. This made him the perfect choice to find the South Magnetic Pole. Ross sailed from Tasmania in November 1840 with two ships, *Erebus* and *Terror*. He knew that the American Charles Wilkes and the Frenchman Dumont d'Urville were using the same route, so he tried farther east. Pushing south through the pack ice, he got to within 80 miles (130 km) of the Antarctic coast. He was stopped by a giant ice shelf, but by then he had found Ross Island, Victoria Land, Mount Erebus (the world's most southerly active volcano), and the position of the South Magnetic Pole.

Magnetic south

AS ROSS SAILED along the coast of Antarctica and through the Ross Sea he took compass readings at different places. When the readings were plotted on a map, from each of the ship's positions, the lines met at one point – the magnetic pole. It lay about 75 miles (120 km) inland, beyond a range of mountains. (See also p 44).

A NEAR DISASTER

13 Mar 1842

In 1841, Ross returned to explore the Great Ice Barrier. Early the next year, in fierce storms, with icebergs all around them, *Erebus* and *Terror* collided. Their rigging became entangled as they were dashed against each other. Only luck and superb seamanship saved them.

Mount Erebus
12,280 ft (3,743 m)

Ross Ice Shelf

Antarctica's Great Ice Barrier
Ross' southward progress was halted by a glistening 196-ft (60-m) high ice cliff – the edge of a vast area of floating ice about the size of France. This barrier was later named the Ross Ice Shelf.

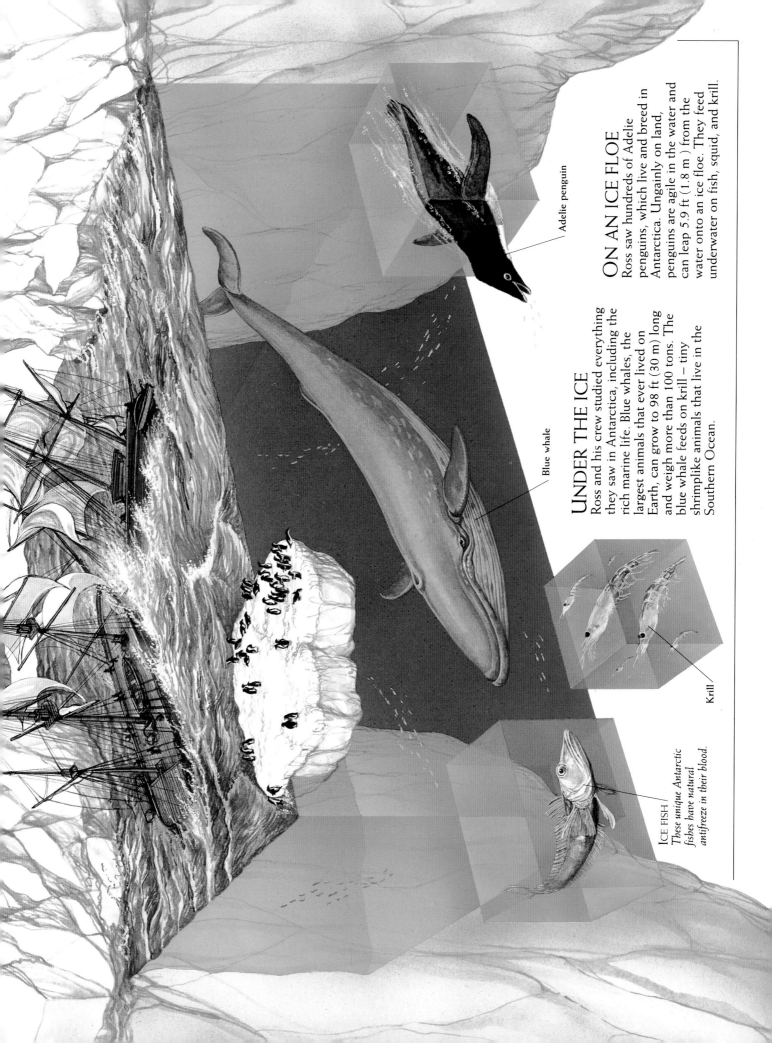

Adelie penguin

ON AN ICE FLOE

Ross saw hundreds of Adelie penguins, which live and breed in Antarctica. Ungainly on land, penguins are agile in the water and can leap 5.9 ft (1.8 m) from the water onto an ice floe. They feed underwater on fish, squid, and krill.

Blue whale

UNDER THE ICE

Ross and his crew studied everything they saw in Antarctica, including the rich marine life. Blue whales, the largest animals that ever lived on Earth, can grow to 98 ft (30 m) long and weigh more than 100 tons. The blue whale feeds on krill – tiny shrimplike animals that live in the Southern Ocean.

Krill

ICE FISH
These unique Antarctic fishes have natural antifreeze in their blood.

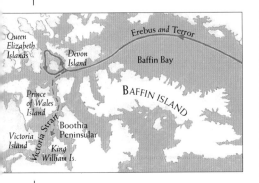

THE LOST EXPEDITION

AT 59, SIR JOHN FRANKLIN WAS OLD FOR a polar explorer, but he had courage. He had fought at the Battle of Trafalgar and explored 5,592 miles (9,000 km) of Canada's Arctic coast between 1819 and 1822. In May 1845, the British Royal Navy sent him to continue the search for a Northwest Passage. His ships, *Erebus* and *Terror*, had proved themselves with Ross in Antarctica, and since then they had been improved. They even had a simple form of central heating in the cabins. By July 26, Franklin's expedition was in Baffin Bay, where they met a whaling boat. The whaler's captain dined aboard *Erebus* with Franklin and his officers. He was the last person to see them alive.

The fatal mistake
Franklin's charts wrongly showed King William Island joined to Boothia Peninsula, so he tried to sail through the ice-choked Victoria Strait. Unknown to him, there was a passable route around the east and south sides of the island.

SINKING SHIPS
22 April 1848
After two winters stuck in the ice, the crews abandoned *Erebus* and *Terror*. The ships probably sank soon afterward.

Ship's lifeboat

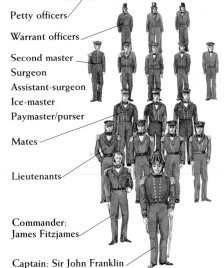

Cabin boys
Royal marines
Able seamen
Petty officers
Warrant officers
Second master
Surgeon
Assistant-surgeon
Ice-master
Paymaster/purser
Mates
Lieutenants
Commander: James Fitzjames
Captain: Sir John Franklin

CREW OF *EREBUS*
Erebus carried 67 men, while the slightly smaller *Terror* carried 62. Both crews were hand-picked. Franklin was the captain of *Erebus*, while Crozier was *Terror*'s captain.

THE LONG MARCH
26 April 1848
Captain Crozier and his men marched south toward Hudson Bay, dragging their supplies on sleds. They took one of the ship's boats in case they had to cross open water.

Was it lead poisoning?

FRANKLIN'S SHIPS carried the latest development in food technology – 8,000 cans of soup, vegetables and meat. But the cans were sealed with lead, and some scientists believe the crews were fatally weakened by lead poisoning.

The frozen man
In 1981, scientists dug up the frozen body of John Torrington, a 20-year-old furnace operator on *Terror*. Tests showed that he had ten times the normal amount of lead in his body.

Canned rations

> "We found, also, a small clothes-brush near, and a horn pocket-comb, in which a few light-brown hairs still remained."
>
> Admiral Sir Leopold McClintock's account of belongings found beside a skeleton in 1859

What happened?

The fate of Franklin's lost expedition has been pieced together over the years. Search parties found skeletons, clothing, and supplies, as well as notes hidden in a grave site. It seems the ships were trapped in ice in the winter of 1846. By April 1848, Franklin and 23 others had died and the ships were breaking up. The remaining men headed south, hoping to reach a trading post on Hudson Bay. All of them perished on the way.

The desperate search
In the 10 years after Sir John Franklin and his crews disappeared, more than 30 expeditions tried to find him or discover his fate. In 1850–1851 the ships *Resolute, Assistance, Intrepid,* and *Pioneer* wintered in the Arctic during their search for clues to the mystery.

ON THEIR LAST LEGS
Close to exhaustion and sick with scurvy, Crozier's men may have bought seal meat from Eskimos.

ESKIMO SEALING PARTY
An Eskimo family hunting seals near the north shore of King William Island claimed to have seen Crozier and his men heading for Great Fish River.

Inuit ingenuity

THE LOCAL INUIT (Eskimos) used steel from Franklin's abandoned ships to make blades for these bone-handled knives, which were found by one of the search parties years later.

Natural materials
Seals, whales, bears, and caribou provided the bone for the handles.

WHO WAS HE?

One of the skeletons found later, close to the boat, was thought to have been an officer "as he had a telescope strapped over his shoulders, and a double-barrelled gun lay underneath him." Was he an officer who broke away from the party to talk to some Eskimos?

UNSUITABLE CLOTHES

European explorers were slow to learn from the Eskimos, whose sealskin clothing was perfectly adapted to the harsh polar environment. It is strange that although Franklin's men wore gloves and helmets, they had only their naval uniforms and sailcloth windbreakers to ward off the Arctic cold.

Weather helmet with flaps

Windbreaker coat over naval uniform

Sealskin and fur gloves

Telescope

Shotgun

Woollen leggings

ENCOUNTER WITH ESKIMOS

Spring 1850?

In 1854, Scottish explorer John Rae met a group of Eskimos who told him, "In the spring, four winters since, while some Eskimo families were killing seals near the north shore of a large island, about 40 white men were seen traveling southward over the ice, dragging a boat and sleds with them..."

Sealskin and fur jacket

Skinning seal with a knife.

THE VOYAGE OF THE *FRAM*

THE NORWEGIAN FRIDTJOF NANSEN WAS the greatest of all Arctic explorers. He decided to design a ship that would withstand the pressure of ice – and so drift toward the North Pole locked in the ice. The design of the ship *Fram* worked perfectly, and she drifted right across the Arctic Ocean. When Nansen realized that she would miss the North Pole, he and Hjalmar Johansen set off on foot. They got to within 236 miles (380 km) of the Pole before they had to turn back.

Fram's route from Norway
Nansen sailed along the Siberian coast before heading into the ice. A year later, he and a companion set out for the North Pole on foot while the *Fram* continued her drift.

24 June 1893 — INTO THE ICE
Nansen left Norway in the *Fram*, taking with him 12 men and 30 dogs. To help her maneuver in the ice, the *Fram* was just 113 ft (34.4 m) long, and 36 ft (11 m) wide at the water line.

20 Sept 1893 — DRIFTING
As planned, Nansen took the ship into pack ice north of Siberia. Each time the pressure of the ice increased, the ship rode up and sat on top of it. When the pressure eased, the ship settled back into the water. The *Fram* drifted like this for 35 months, while her crew studied the weather, marine life, and ocean currents.

EYEWITNESS
"Beautiful weather for the last few days; the moon transforms the whole of this ice world into a fairyland."
Fridtjof Nansen from his book *Farthest North*, 1897

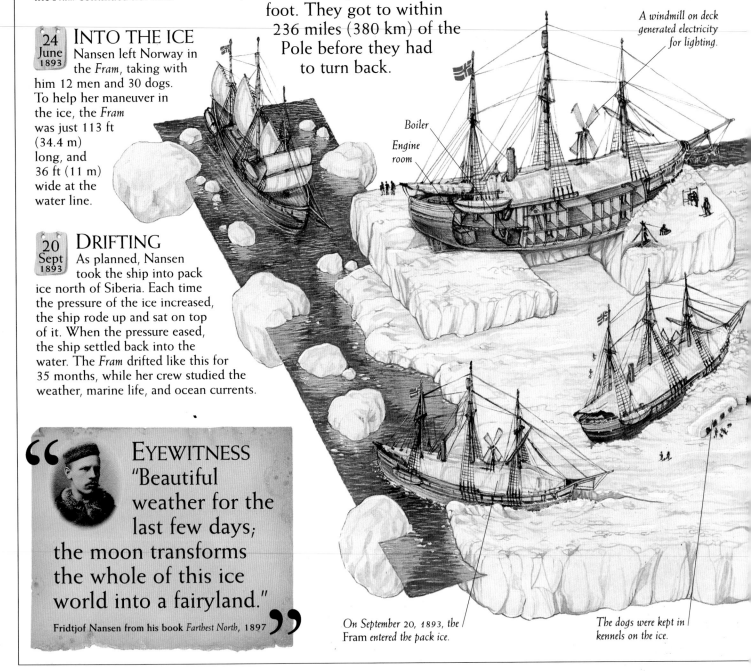

A windmill on deck generated electricity for lighting.

Boiler

Engine room

On September 20, 1893, the *Fram* entered the pack ice.

The dogs were kept in kennels on the ice.

FREE AT LAST!

13 Aug 1896

The *Fram* broke free of the ice and reached open sea. A week later she arrived on the Norwegian coast.

FARTHEST NORTH
Nansen planted the Norwegian flag at 86° 14'N, the farthest north anyone had ever been.

SOUTH TO SAFETY
The two men tied their kayaks together and sailed to Franz Josef Land.

ACROSS THE WATER
The two remaining dogs and the equipment were ferried across open water in the kayaks.

OVER THE ICE
Nansen and Johansen set off across the ice on skis, with kayaks, sleds, 28 dogs, and food for 100 days.

WINTERING IN THE ARCTIC
Nansen and Johansen spent their second Arctic winter in a stone hut on one of the Franz Josef islands. They lived on bear and seal meat. Next spring they moved south through the islands.

HEROES

25 Aug 1896

After four months on the ice and a second winter in Franz Josef Land, Nansen and Johansen were amazed to meet an English expedition, whose ship *Windward* took them back to Norway. A week later the two men and the crew of the *Fram* were reunited in Trömso, where they were welcomed as heroes.

Arctic poppies
As Nansen and Johansen sailed through the islands in early summer, Franz Josef Land was covered with bright yellow poppies.

Strange meeting
On June 17, 1896, in the silent world of rock and ice, Nansen thought he heard a dog bark. Minutes later he was shaking hands with the English explorer Frederick Jackson of the *Windward* expedition.

A slippery solution

THE *FRAM* (Norwegian for "forward") was specially designed for ice. She was built by a Scottish shipbuilder called Colin Archer, who lived in Norway. His idea was that "the whole craft should be able to slip like an eel out of the embraces of the ice."

Oak and iron beams stopped the Fram's sides being crushed by ice.

Under pressure the ship rose like a bar of soap being squeezed.

The Fram sat on the ice until it moved, releasing her into the water.

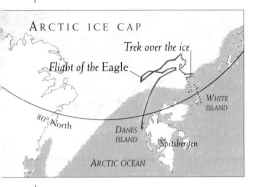

ARCTIC ICE CAP

Trek over the ice

Flight of the Eagle

WHITE ISLAND

80° North

DANES ISLAND

Spitsbergen

ARCTIC OCEAN

Andrée's ill-fated journey
Andrée's plan was to float straight across the Arctic Ocean, taking photographs that would later be used to make maps. He set off from Danes Island, to the west of the Norwegian island of Spitsbergen. His journey ended on the Arctic sea ice.

TRICKY OPERATION

Filling a hydrogen balloon is dangerous, because the gas is highly explosive. The balloon house had wood and canvas walls that were designed to collapse outward if there was an explosion.

THREE
MEN IN A BALLOON

ON SUNDAY, JULY 11, 1897, A HYDROGEN balloon took off from the shores of Danes Island in the Arctic in an attempt to cross over the North Pole. The leader of the expedition, Swedish balloonist Salomon Andrée, was an experienced Arctic traveler. His companions were Nils Strindberg, a scientist, and Knut Fraenkel, an engineer. They took food, fuel for the stove, tents, rifles, a boat, and sleds so that they could cross the ice if the balloon was forced to land. The launch team watched as the balloon, *Eagle*, rose and headed north. It was never seen again.

Balloon in collapsible structure called a balloon house.

11 July 1897 LIFTOFF Instead of rising cleanly, the balloon dragged along the rocks, trailing its mooring ropes and damaging its steering gear beyond repair.

SO FAR, SO GOOD
A carrier pigeon released before the crash carried an "All well" message to a Norwegian fishing boat.

Light, strong, and full of gas

THE TOP HALF of the balloon was made of three double layers of Chinese silk, varnished inside and out. The lower half had one double layer to save weight. The *Eagle* had to be large enough to hold gas for a month and carry three men, their supplies, and equipment – a load of 6,614 lb (3,000 kg). The filled balloon held 169,500 cubic ft (4,800 cubic meters) of hydrogen gas.

Inspecting the balloon canopy for leaks

One layer of varnish

Three double layers of silk cloth

One layer of varnish

Balloon construction

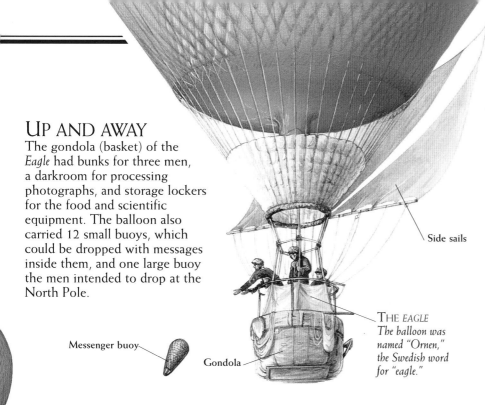

UP AND AWAY

The gondola (basket) of the *Eagle* had bunks for three men, a darkroom for processing photographs, and storage lockers for the food and scientific equipment. The balloon also carried 12 small buoys, which could be dropped with messages inside them, and one large buoy the men intended to drop at the North Pole.

Messenger buoy

Gondola

Side sails

THE EAGLE
The balloon was named "Ornen," the Swedish word for "eagle."

A ROUGH LANDING

14 July 1897

Three days after takeoff, the expedition ran into freezing fog. The balloon was weighed down by ice, and the gondola scraped across the frozen ground until it finally crashed. It had traveled only 516 miles (830 km). As the *Eagle* lost height, the men threw out all the ballast and over 485 lb (220 kg) of food in a desperate attempt to stay airborne. It didn't work, but at least they survived the crash landing.

DEFLATED BALLOON
The balloon lay in a crumpled heap on the ice. There was no hope of getting it up in the air again.

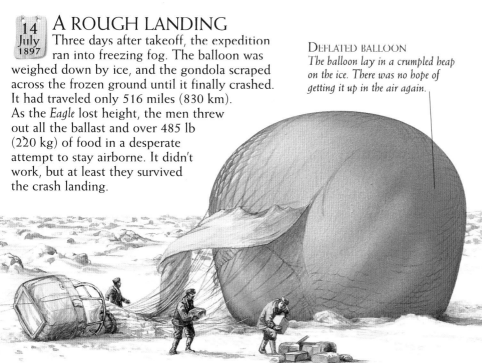

How did they die?

The men trekked across the ice for two months, but all three died soon after reaching White Island, east of Spitsbergen. Their supplies were low, but it is unlikely that they starved because bear meat was found at their camp. Some people think they were poisoned by carbon monoxide from their cooking stove. A Norwegian sealer had another theory: "I think they died in their sleep. The cold finished them off."

Thirty years on

IN AUGUST 1930, more than 30 years after *Eagle* disappeared, two Norwegian sailors found the remains of the balloonists' final camp on White Island. The bodies of the explorers were taken back to Sweden, together with diaries and a camera. When the photos were developed, they showed the men pulling sleds, camping, and hunting on the ice. The diaries told the rest of the sad story.

Camping on ice
One photograph, developed later in Stockholm, shows the three men camping on the ice, with the upturned boat they would later use to reach White Island.

Hunting and hauling
Two more photographs found in the camera showed Fraenkel and Strindberg with a polar bear they had killed for food (above), and Fraenkel, Andrée, and Strindberg pushing a sled with the boat on it across a wall of high ice (below).

The Quest for the Poles

T HE FIRST 20 YEARS of the twentieth century are sometimes called "The Heroic Age of Polar Exploration." The Northwest Passage had been navigated in 1906, and by that time most of Antarctica's coastline had been mapped. Explorers now turned toward the two great challenges that remained – the conquest of the North and South Poles.

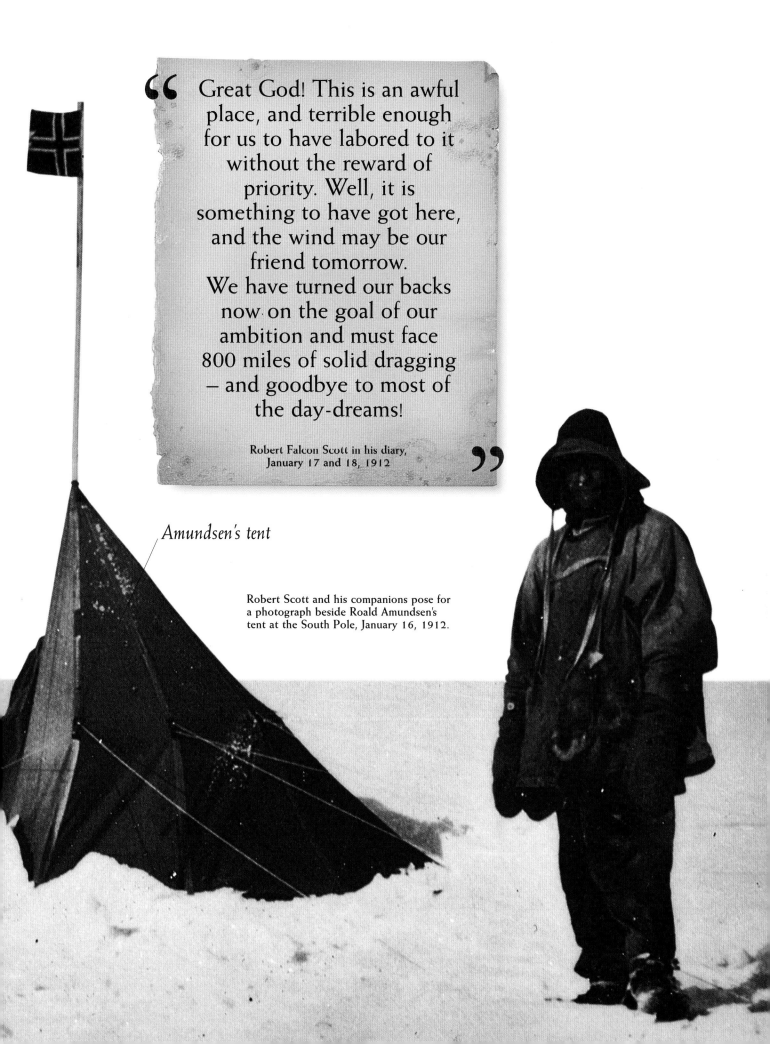

> " Great God! This is an awful place, and terrible enough for us to have labored to it without the reward of priority. Well, it is something to have got here, and the wind may be our friend tomorrow. We have turned our backs now on the goal of our ambition and must face 800 miles of solid dragging – and goodbye to most of the day-dreams! "
>
> Robert Falcon Scott in his diary,
> January 17 and 18, 1912

Amundsen's tent

Robert Scott and his companions pose for a photograph beside Roald Amundsen's tent at the South Pole, January 16, 1912.

"The Pole at last"
Peary's companions on the dash to the Pole were his partner Matthew Henson, and four Inuit men – Egingwah, Ootah, Seegloo, and Ooqueah. Peary took this photograph of them on April 6, 1909, at the spot he claimed was the North Pole.

ACROSS THE TOP OF THE WORLD

ROBERT PEARY, A CIVIL ENGINEER IN THE US Navy, had a burning ambition – to conquer the North Pole. In 1886, at age 30, he made his first polar journey, exploring the icy interior of Greenland by sled. Over the next 23 years he explored and mapped the north coast of Greenland and tried several times to reach the North Pole – getting to within 274 miles (280 km) in 1905–6 in his ship *Roosevelt*. In March 1909, with Matthew Henson, 50 Inuit (Eskimo) helpers, and 250 dogs, Peary crossed harsh terrain before making a final 36-day trek to the Pole.

COLD ENOUGH TO BURN
Traveling in temperatures as low as -58° F (-50° C), Peary wrote, "The bitter wind burned our faces so that they cracked. Even the Eskimos complained of their noses. The air was as keen and bitter as frozen steel."

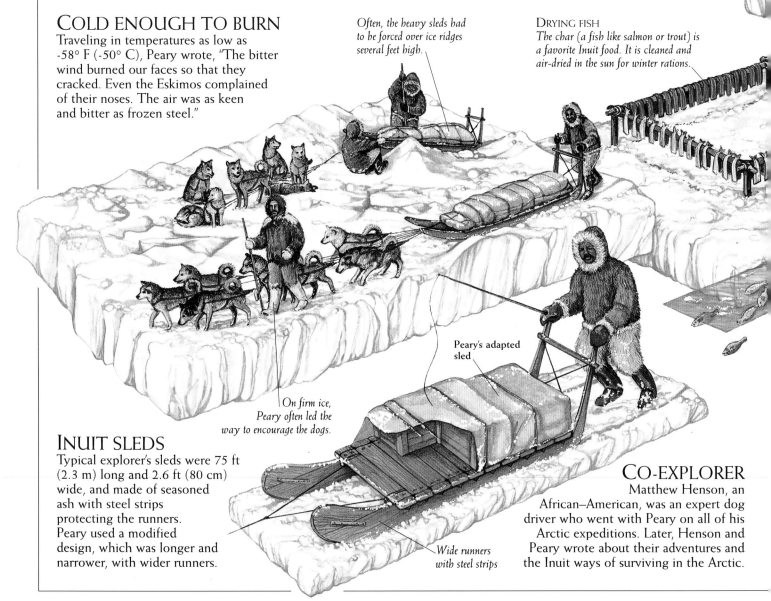

Often, the heavy sleds had to be forced over ice ridges several feet high.

DRYING FISH
The char (a fish like salmon or trout) is a favorite Inuit food. It is cleaned and air-dried in the sun for winter rations.

On firm ice, Peary often led the way to encourage the dogs.

Peary's adapted sled

INUIT SLEDS
Typical explorer's sleds were 75 ft (2.3 m) long and 2.6 ft (80 cm) wide, and made of seasoned ash with steel strips protecting the runners. Peary used a modified design, which was longer and narrower, with wider runners.

Wide runners with steel strips

CO-EXPLORER
Matthew Henson, an African–American, was an expert dog driver who went with Peary on all of his Arctic expeditions. Later, Henson and Peary wrote about their adventures and the Inuit ways of surviving in the Arctic.

LEARNING INUIT WAYS

Peary realized that the key to success was to learn from the Inuit, so he assembled a team of Inuit helpers. The first winter they spent hunting bear and caribou to make smoked meat for the journey, while the women made boots and clothes from seal, caribou, and wolf skins.

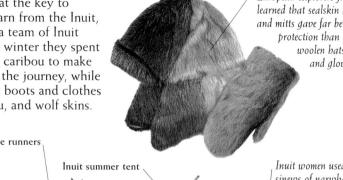

SEAL WARMTH
European explorers finally learned that sealskin hoods and mitts gave far better protection than woolen hats and gloves.

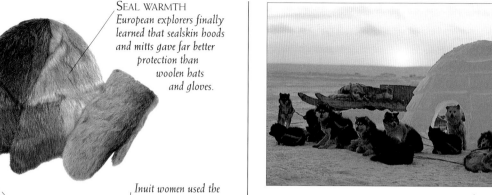

Dome home
Peary's Inuit support teams went ahead to make a trail and build small igloos for overnight shelters. Sometimes, on such journeys, igloos were made for the dogs, too. The igloos were made by placing snow blocks in a spiral upward, leaving a small ventilation hole at the top.

Rolling sledge runners

Eight-man tent used by Peary's party

Inuit summer tent

Inuit women used the sinews of narwhal (a type of whale) to sew skins.

Inuit hunters shot caribou and brought them back to the camp.

Shoals of dying halibut, trapped beneath the ice, are easy prey for the Inuit.

Making ice runners

WHERE DRIFTWOOD was scarce, the Inuit made runners for their sleds from frozen fish and rolled-up caribou skins.

1 Fishes rolled in caribou skins were trodden into a long sausage shape.

2 The rolls of frozen caribou skin were given a good coating of moss and slush.

3 Water poured on to the layer of moss and slush, instantly froze to hard ice.

Back home

Of all the great polar journeys, the race to the North Pole stands out because of the huge controversy that erupted over the rival claims of Robert Peary and Frederick Cook. On Peary's return from the Arctic in 1909, he was furious to learn that Cook, once a friend but now a rival, was claiming he had reached the Pole a year earlier – on April 21, 1908 – but had been forced to winter in the Arctic. After a long investigation, the US Congress backed Peary's claim, promoted him to the rank of Rear-Admiral, and gave him a pension. However, even today, there are many people who wonder if Peary really did reach the North Pole.

Polar punch-up
The world was fascinated by the disagreement between Peary and Cook. Newspaper cartoons (like this French one) made the most of it!

RACE TO THE SOUTH POLE

IN THE YEAR 1911 TWO EXPEDITIONS SET out in a bid to be first to reach the South Pole. One was led by Captain Robert Scott, a British naval officer. The other was led by Roald Amundsen, the great Norwegian explorer The two men's plans could not have been more different. While Scott decided to travel on skis, hauling his sleds across the ice, Amundsen – an expert skier – traveled fast and light, using dog teams to pull the heavy sleds. Both parties reached the Pole, but only one of them made it back.

Scott's hut
During the winter of 1911, Scott's party made the hut at Cape Evans on Ross Island their home. Today, the inside of the hut is just as the men left it.

11 Jan 1911 — AMUNDSEN'S BASE

Amundsen built his camp on the Ross Ice Shelf and named the hut "Framheim" after the ship *Fram* he had borrowed from Fridtjof Nansen (see pages 16-17). With him he had 8 men and 118 sled dogs.

21 Dec 1911 — UP AND OVER

After struggling through deep snow, Scott's men reached the top of the Beardmore Glacier with their equipment.

5 Nov 1911 — SCOTT'S START

After several months at Cape Evans, Scott set off with 32 men, 33 sled dogs, 17 ponies, and two motorized tractor sleds. Both sleds broke down crossing the Ross Ice Shelf.

Scott's journey

MERCY KILLING
At the foot of the glacier, the remaining ponies were exhausted and had to be shot.

Scott's base camp at Cape Evans

Motorized tractor-sled

SELF–SACRIFICE
Crippled by frostbite, Oates walked to his death in a blizzard rather than slow down his companions.

29 Mar 1912 — LAST WORDS

Scott, Wilson, and Bowers died in their tent, totally exhausted. Scott's last diary entry, on March 29, says, "It seems a pity but I do not think I can write more." Then, a final thought for those back home, "For God's sake look after our people." When the men were found, Scott's diary was under his arm.

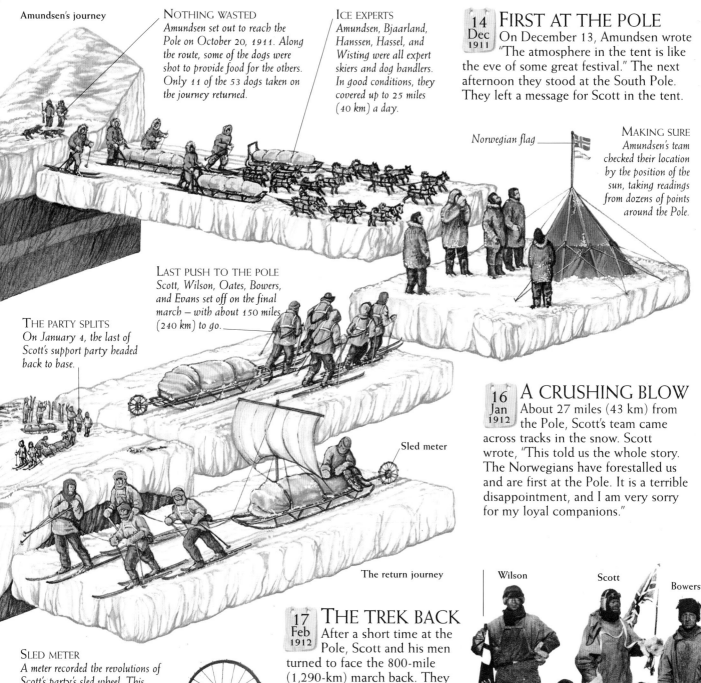

Amundsen's journey

NOTHING WASTED
Amundsen set out to reach the Pole on October 20, 1911. Along the route, some of the dogs were shot to provide food for the others. Only 11 of the 53 dogs taken on the journey returned.

ICE EXPERTS
Amundsen, Bjaarland, Hanssen, Hassel, and Wisting were all expert skiers and dog handlers. In good conditions, they covered up to 25 miles (40 km) a day.

LAST PUSH TO THE POLE
Scott, Wilson, Oates, Bowers, and Evans set off on the final march – with about 150 miles (240 km) to go.

THE PARTY SPLITS
On January 4, the last of Scott's support party headed back to base.

Sled meter

The return journey

SLED METER
A meter recorded the revolutions of Scott's party's sled wheel. This showed how far they had traveled.

14 Dec 1911 FIRST AT THE POLE

On December 13, Amundsen wrote "The atmosphere in the tent is like the eve of some great festival." The next afternoon they stood at the South Pole. They left a message for Scott in the tent.

Norwegian flag

MAKING SURE
Amundsen's team checked their location by the position of the sun, taking readings from dozens of points around the Pole.

16 Jan 1912 A CRUSHING BLOW

About 27 miles (43 km) from the Pole, Scott's team came across tracks in the snow. Scott wrote, "This told us the whole story. The Norwegians have forestalled us and are first at the Pole. It is a terrible disappointment, and I am very sorry for my loyal companions."

17 Feb 1912 THE TREK BACK

After a short time at the Pole, Scott and his men turned to face the 800-mile (1,290-km) march back. They were hungry, suffering from frostbite, and slowed down by deep snow. On February 17, Evans collapsed and died.

Wilson   Scott   Bowers

Evans   Oates

Haggard faces tell the story
At the Pole, Scott's party built a cairn (pile of snow blocks used as a marker), hoisted their flag, and took photographs. Scott wrote in his diary, "None of us slept much after the shock of our discovery."

TWO JOURNEYS

Scott was very unlucky with the weather conditions. Almost from the start his expedition became a desperate fight for survival. By contrast, Amundsen's team, whose base was 60 miles (100 km) nearer the Pole, were able to make the most of the better conditions they met and their expertise as dog drivers.

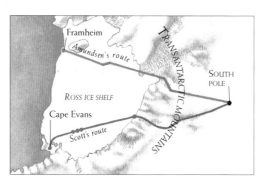

Framheim

Amundsen's route

TRANSANTARCTIC MOUNTAINS

SOUTH POLE

ROSS ICE SHELF

Cape Evans

Scott's route

escape in the history of polar exploration. Shackleton left South Georgia, an island in the South Atlantic Ocean, on December 5, 1914. At first *Endurance* made good progress, pushing her way through narrow channels ("leads") in the pack ice, and skirting around icebergs that towered above her decks. But on January 18, 1915, the wind shifted, closing the leads and packing the ice floes around the ship. She was stuck tight. During the long dark winter the pack ice carried the ship almost 600 miles (1,000 km) north. Finally her huge timbers snapped like matchsticks and icy water flooded into the holds, forcing the men to abandon ship. For the next six months the crew camped on drifting ice floes they named Ocean Camp and Patience Camp.

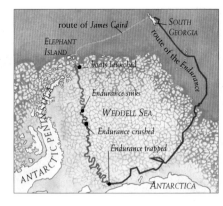

Shackleton's route south
The *Endurance* left the island of South Georgia in the South Atlantic Ocean, in November 1914. She sank a year later, after being crushed by ice.

Seal blubber was used as fuel for the stove.

OUT TO DRY
The men dried their clothes on lines rigged across the ice.

WINTER NIGHTS
Huddled in their tents, the men played cards and read aloud.

The motion of the ice made some men seasick.

Tents were collapsed for packing.

TIME TO GO
When the men abandoned Patience Camp it was little more than a raft of rotting ice.

CRACK UP!
When Ocean Camp became unsafe, the men set up a new one on another ice floe. They called this camp "Patience Camp" because they had no choice but to wait for the ice to break up and free them. After three-and-a-half months the floe cracked and the crew hurriedly launched their boats.

ESCAPE FROM THE ICE
12 April 1916 As they left Patience Camp, the boats were spattered with bird droppings. It was the start of a difficult six-day journey across the Southern Ocean to Elephant Island.

Midwinter celebration
Halfway through the Antarctic winter, on June 22, Shackleton and his crew held a dinner on board *Endurance*. The room they nicknamed "the Ritz" was decorated with flags and bunting.

THE GREAT ESCAPE

IN 1914, SIR ERNEST SHACKLETON SET out to cross Antarctica from coast to coast, a journey of 2,025 miles (3,300 km) Although his ship *Endurance* was wrecked before he set foot in Antarctica, he and his men pulled off the greatest

STUCK!

18 Jan 1915 As howling gales drove ice against the ship, the crew tried to free her using steam and sail.

The crew unloaded supplies down a canvas ramp.

CAMPING ON ICE

The months spent at Ocean Camp were hard. It was now summer, and the men's clothes and sleeping bags were always soaked through.

ABANDON SHIP!

27 Oct 1915 Shackleton knew *Endurance* was doomed. The crushing ice had lifted the ship almost out of the water and forced her onto her side. He later wrote, "Huge blocks of ice, weighing many tons, were lifted into the air and tossed aside. We were helpless intruders in a strange world." Reluctantly, Shackleton gave the order to abandon ship.

A LONG HARD HAUL
Lifeboats were hauled over the ice ridges and deep snow on sleds.

THE HUNTER HUNTED

There were many dangers on the ice. While out hunting seals and penguins, one of the men nearly became dinner for an enormous leopard seal.

The aim of the expedition
Mawson's plan was to chart the 2,000-mile (3,200-km) stretch of unexplored Antarctic coastline that lay directly south of Australia.

CAPE DENISON
8 Jan 1912 Mawson's ship *Aurora* landed the 18-man main party on a rocky headland they named Cape Denison. An 8-man party was also put ashore 1,500 miles (2,410 km) farther along the coast.

THE LONELIEST MARCH
IN 1912, ON THE GALE-SWEPT COAST of Adelie Land, Australian geologist Douglas Mawson survived one of the worst journeys ever made in Antarctica. The expedition landed at Commonwealth Bay in January, and the men erected their hut in fierce winds. During the winter they recorded high wind speeds as they waited for spring and the start of the sledding season. In November, Mawson, Xavier Mertz, and Lieutenant B.E.S Ninnis set out to explore the unknown area to the east of their camp. The journey was to turn into a nightmare.

WINDBREAKERS
The two base huts were built in pyramid shapes so that the wind would blow right over them.

SMALL BUT TOUGH
The Aurora was a 660-ton (600-metric-ton) sealing vessel, strengthened for working in pack ice.

DUAL PURPOSE
With its wings removed, Mawson's Vickers plane was used as a tractor. It towed sleds of supplies from the main base to the depot at Aladdin's Cave.

Food was often stockpiled under a mound of snow called a cairn.

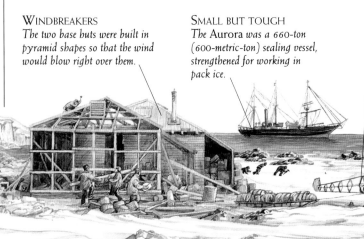

RELIEF!
On January 29, 1913, Mawson found food and directions to Aladdin's Cave at a cairn. The cave was also stocked with food.

Sledding rations

BEFORE A SLEDDING PARTY set out, provisions were carefully weighed and then packed in canvas bags, each one containing food allowances for three men for a week. Only one bag was to be opened each week.

Bags containing weekly rations

ALADDIN'S CAVE
1 Feb 1913 The cairn left by the search party saved Mawson's life. The food gave him enough strength to reach Aladdin's Cave – just in time. Blizzards trapped him there for a week. If he had been caught in the open he would have perished. At last a lull in the storm gave him a chance to trek the last few miles to base. The *Aurora* had just left, but five men had stayed behind to search for him.

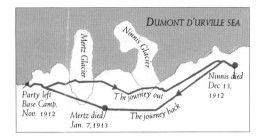

DUMONT D'URVILLE SEA

Mertz Glacier

Ninnis Glacier

Ninnis died
Dec 13,
1912

Party left
Base Camp,
Nov. 1912

The journey out

Mertz died
Jan. 7, 1913

The journey back

THE EASTERN PARTY

Six separate exploration teams set out from the main base. Two went south, one went west, and three, including Mawson's team, pushed eastward.

Technological "firsts"

MAWSON MADE USE OF the new technologies of the time. As well as taking the first airplane to Antarctica, he was also the first explorer to take radios there.

Remote radio station
By using a relay station (right) on Macquarie Island, 850 miles (1,370 km) south of Tasmania, the expedition was able to radio messages to Australia.

ON THE MOVE

10 Nov 1912 Mawson, Mertz, and Ninnis set off to explore the land to the east. One man walked ahead to choose the route and encourage the dogs. He was followed by one team pulling two light sleds, then the other team pulling a third sled.

CLOSE TO THE EDGE
Crossing the Mertz Glacier, the men were delayed several times when dogs or sleds fell part way into crevasses.

TOUGH GOING
The Ninnis Glacier was an expanse of ice, crevasses, and steep ridges of wind-packed snow called "sastrugi."

DISASTER STRIKES

14 Dec 1912 The men were over 310 miles (500 km) from base when the snow bridge over a large crevasse gave way under the last sled. When Mawson and Mertz turned to look back, Ninnis, along with his dogs and sled, was nowhere to be seen.

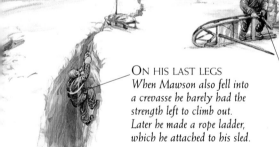

ON HIS LAST LEGS
When Mawson also fell into a crevasse he barely had the strength left to climb out. Later he made a rope ladder, which he attached to his sled.

HEADING HOME ALONE
Mawson buried Mertz beneath a snow cairn. He cut his sled in half with a penknife to save weight, then he continued on his journey.

When Mertz fell ill, Mawson pulled him along on the sled.

Ninnis and the dogs fell headlong into a deep crevasse.

> For hours I lay in the bag, rolling over in my mind all that lay behind and the chance of the future. I seemed to stand alone.

Sir Douglas Mawson from his book
The Home of the Blizzard, 1915

DOUBLE TRAGEDY

Mawson and Mertz headed back with a makeshift tent and a few rations. The dogs, fed at first on old sealskin mitts, were killed and eaten when they were too weak to go on. The men were also weakening. On January 7, 1913 Mertz died in his sleep after several fits.

A devastating loss
For hours Mawson and Mertz called down the crevasse, hoping for a sign of life from Ninnis. There was none. Along with their friend, they had lost their tent and most of their food.

"In the event of my not surviving the boat journey to South Georgia you will do your best for the rescue of the party. You are in full command from the time the boat leaves this island."

Ernest Shackleton's orders to Frank Wild before leaving Elephant Island, April 23, 1916

ELEPHANT ISLAND

18 April 1916

After six days at sea, the men scrambled ashore on a small rocky beach on Elephant Island. It was the first dry land they had stood on since they left South Georgia 16 months earlier. They were soaked to the skin and half-starved, but at least they were safe.

THE SNUGGERY

The men built a hut from two boats placed upside down on stone walls. They were packed inside like "sardines in a tin." On the island they had fresh water, elephant seals, and penguins to provide food and fuel.

STAYING IN TOUCH

On the stormy crossing to Elephant Island the crews of the three boats – *Stancomb Wills*, *Dudley Docker*, and *James Caird* – fought hard to stay together. At any moment the boats could have been swamped by huge waves.

FAREWELL

24 April 1916

Six days after arriving at Elephant Island, Shackleton set sail in the 20-ft (6-m) *James Caird* with five companions. The nearest help lay at the whaling stations on South Georgia, 800 miles (1,300 km) away across the world's stormiest ocean. The men had to try and reach them. The ship's carpenter made a wood and canvas deck for the boat, which the men could crawl under to avoid the wind and spray. They took food for a month and two barrels of fresh water.

Sitting it out

The men left behind on Elephant Island suffered great hardship. When the seals and penguins left the island at the end of the summer, their stock of food and fuel soon ran low. Finally, they were forced to eat seaweed, limpets (a mollusk), and soup made of boiled seal bones. They had barely two days' food left when Shackleton, on board the ship *Yelcho*, arrived to rescue them.

ALL AT SEA

On the journey out through the pack ice the men slept in the boats. Occasionally, a large ice floe provided a steady place for the cook to prepare a hot meal for the hungry men.

A ROUGH CROSSING

For 17 days the crew of the *James Caird* worked four-hour shifts, three at a time. Those off duty tried to rest in the cramped wet space below deck.

STORM AT SEA
When the wind eased, the men fought to break off the layers of ice that threatened to capsize the boat.

BAILING OUT
In one squall the boat was almost engulfed by the biggest wave they had ever seen, and the sea anchor broke away.

The sea anchor was made from three oars and a piece of canvas.

Vincent and McNeish were too weak to travel, so McCarthy was left with them while the other three set off across the mountains.

Shackleton used the axe to cut steps and ledges in the ice.

AN INCREDIBLE JOURNEY

Despite violent storms that almost sank their boat, the six men reached South Georgia in 17 days. But they had landed on the wrong side of the island. Between them and the whaling station at Stromness lay a range of mountains that had never been crossed. With just a makeshift axe and a short length of rope, Worsley, Shackleton, and Crean climbed over the mountains in 36 hours.

20 May 1916 SLIDING HOME

Holding on to one another like three tobogganers, the men slid down a snowfield to safety. A short time later, they staggered into the whaling station. They had made it.

All safe, all well
On August 30, 1916, after four failed rescue attempts, the Chilean naval ship *Yelcho* picked up Shackleton's men on Elephant Island. Not one life was lost on the expedition.

FLYING OVER THE POLES

IN THE 1920S, POLAR EXPLORERS started using a new technology – air transportation. Airships and planes, which had been developed during the First World War, offered explorers an ideal way to map the polar regions. In 1926, Richard Byrd and Floyd Bennett of the US Navy flew to the North Pole in a Fokker monoplane. Later the same year, the Italian Umberto Nobile flew the airship *Norge* across the North Pole. In 1928, Australian Hubert Wilkins made the first flights in Antarctica, and soon after that Richard Byrd flew over the South Pole (1929). Another American, Lincoln Ellsworth, made the first flight across the Antarctic continent in 1935.

Scott's balloon
In 1902, Englishman Robert Scott was lifted 600 ft (180 m) above the Ross Ice Shelf in a hydrogen-filled balloon. From that height he could see the peaks and glaciers of the Trans-Antarctic Mountain Range, which stood between him and the Pole.

GREENLAND

WELL EQUIPPED
The Dorniers had 360 hp Rolls-Royce engines and the latest navigation equipment. The planes cost Ellsworth $85,000.

Air-speed measuring device

EYEWITNESS
"There, dead ahead of us, and only a few yards away, loomed the twenty-foot hummock of ice. We were headed straight toward it."

Roald Amundsen from his book
My Life as an Explorer, 1927

CLOSE ENCOUNTER
In 1925, Roald Amundsen (left) and Lincoln Ellsworth attempted to fly to the North Pole in two Dornier flying boats designed to land on water or snow. They got within 136 miles (220 km) of the Pole, landed on a patch of open water, abandoned one plane, and flew back in the other.

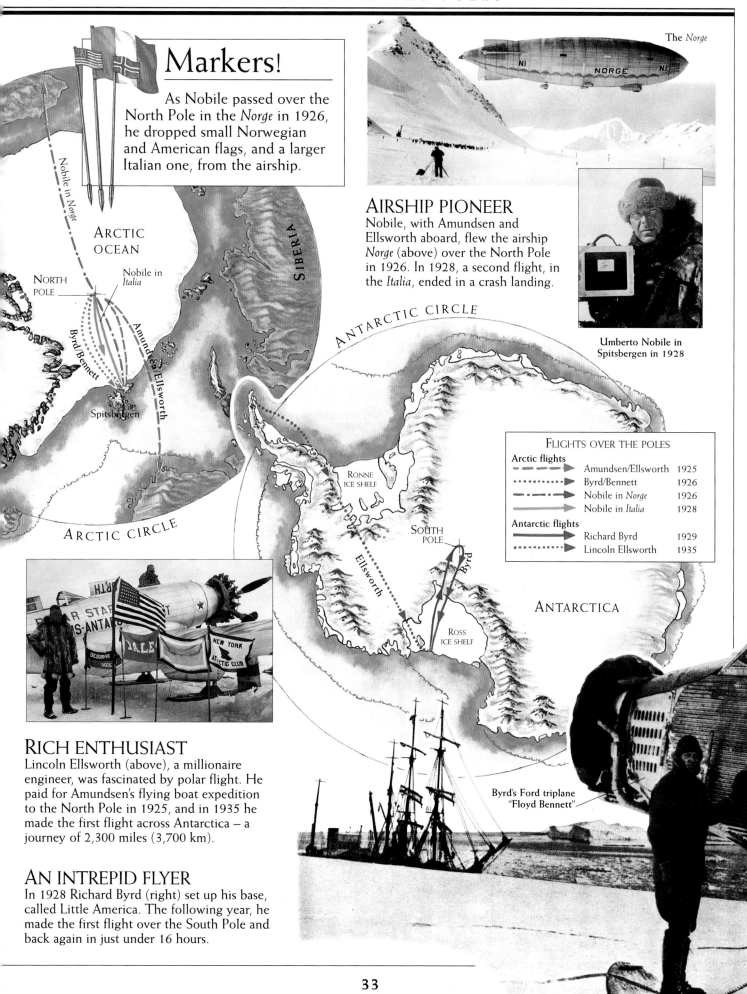

The Norge

Markers!

As Nobile passed over the North Pole in the _Norge_ in 1926, he dropped small Norwegian and American flags, and a larger Italian one, from the airship.

AIRSHIP PIONEER

Nobile, with Amundsen and Ellsworth aboard, flew the airship _Norge_ (above) over the North Pole in 1926. In 1928, a second flight, in the _Italia_, ended in a crash landing.

Umberto Nobile in Spitsbergen in 1928

ARCTIC OCEAN

SIBERIA

Nobile in _Norge_

NORTH POLE

Nobile in _Italia_

Byrd/Bennett

Amundsen Ellsworth

Spitsbergen

ARCTIC CIRCLE

ANTARCTIC CIRCLE

RONNE ICE SHELF

SOUTH POLE

Ellsworth

Byrd

ROSS ICE SHELF

ANTARCTICA

FLIGHTS OVER THE POLES

Arctic flights

⇢	Amundsen/Ellsworth	1925
⇢	Byrd/Bennett	1926
⇢	Nobile in _Norge_	1926
⇢	Nobile in _Italia_	1928

Antarctic flights

→	Richard Byrd	1929
⇢	Lincoln Ellsworth	1935

Byrd's Ford triplane "Floyd Bennett"

RICH ENTHUSIAST

Lincoln Ellsworth (above), a millionaire engineer, was fascinated by polar flight. He paid for Amundsen's flying boat expedition to the North Pole in 1925, and in 1935 he made the first flight across Antarctica – a journey of 2,300 miles (3,700 km).

AN INTREPID FLYER

In 1928 Richard Byrd (right) set up his base, called Little America. The following year, he made the first flight over the South Pole and back again in just under 16 hours.

Atmospheric scientist at New Zealand's Scott Base on Ross Island, Antarctic summer 1994–5.

Hydrogen-filled balloons enable meteorologists (weather experts) to calculate wind speed and direction.

The Scientific Age

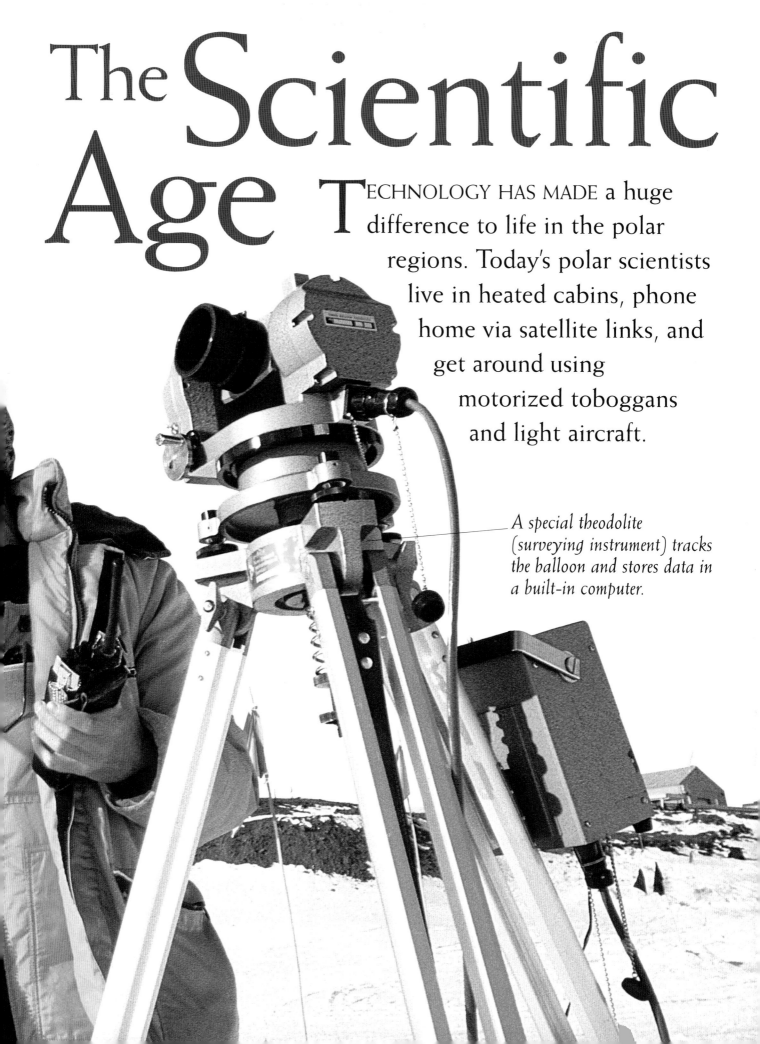

TECHNOLOGY HAS MADE a huge difference to life in the polar regions. Today's polar scientists live in heated cabins, phone home via satellite links, and get around using motorized toboggans and light aircraft.

A special theodolite (surveying instrument) tracks the balloon and stores data in a built-in computer.

A CONTINENT FOR SCIENCE

IN 1957–8, BRITISH GEOLOGIST VIVIAN Fuchs led the first successful expedition across Antarctica via the South Pole. The Trans-Antarctic Expedition took place during a scientific project called the International Geophysical Year. The men used tracked vehicles as well as dog teams, and aircraft on skis flew food and fuel to supply dumps (depots) along the route. Fuchs led the main party overland from the Weddell Sea. Edmund Hillary (one of the first men to climb Mount Everest) crossed the polar plateau from the Ross Sea. When the two parties met and returned to Hillary's base, they had achieved Shackleton's dream of an Antarctic crossing (see page 28).

"As the party moved towards the Pole, I looked back and thought our convoy a brave sight: the orange "Cats" and Weasel (tractor), together with the loaded sleds, bearing fluttering flags of different colors."

Sir Vivian Fuchs from his book
The Crossing of Antarctica, 1958

Fuchs and Hillary
In the photograph above, Vivian Fuchs (left) and New Zealander Edmund Hillary prepare a meal in their tent. A sled-ration box makes a handy table for their belongings. The men's faces have been burned by the fierce sunlight and the intense glare from the snow and ice.

SOUTH ICE
On Christmas Day 1957 the crossing party set out from the advance base called "South Ice," which had been set up 300 miles (480 km) inland. The hut sections and tons of food, fuel, and equipment had been flown in earlier in the year.

MEETING UP
Hillary flew to Depot 700 to join Fuchs for the journey to Scott Base. Fuchs had covered 520 miles (840 km) from the Pole in 15 days. He was now 1,427 miles (2,296 km) from Shackleton Base with 700 miles (1,130 km) to go.

Hillary's depot-laying route from Scott Base onto the polar plateau.

Ice

Bedrock

Depot 700

HALF WAY THERE
Fuchs' party spent four days at the US's Amundsen–Scott Base at the South Pole, servicing the tractors for the second stage of the journey.

Polar plateau

Fuchs' route across the continent.

South Ice

The single-engined Otter made 20 flights to South Ice carrying a ton of supplies each time.

Sno-cat

The hut was built in a pit and snow was allowed to drift over it.

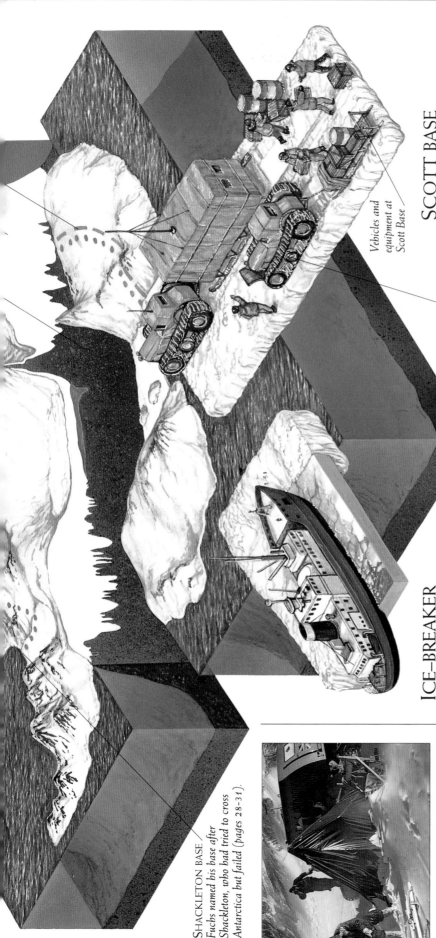

Wing-mounted radar

SCOTT BASE

Hillary made his base, called Scott Base, at Pram Point on Ross Island. Once the tractors, huts, and stores were unloaded, the men set up food and fuel depots along the route to the Pole for Fuchs's crossing party to use.

Vehicles and equipment at Scott Base

TRACTOR
Hillary's modified Ferguson tractors hauled tons of food and fuel to the plateau depots.

"IGY" IN ANTARCTICA

Twelve nations occupied bases in Antarctica during IGY: Argentina, Australia, Belgium, Chile, France, Japan, New Zealand, Norway, South Africa, UK, US, USSR.

SEE-THROUGH ICE

Fuchs' expedition measured the thickness of the ice by setting off explosives in holes in the ice and recording the echoes. Modern methods use airborne radar (right).

IGY Bases in Antarctica

Line shows cutaway on main picture.

ICE-BREAKER

The US ice-breaker *Glacier* made a channel through the ice so that the New Zealanders' supply ship *Endeavour* could get close enough to land the expedition's stores and tractors.

SHACKLETON BASE
Fuchs named his base after Shackleton, who had tried to cross Antarctica but failed (pages 28–31).

Every man to his task

Setting up camp is a highly organized routine. While "outside men" anchor the tent and secure the sleds and other equipment, "inside men" unpack the sleeping bags and light the stoves.

FACT file

- International Geophysical Year (IGY) involved 67 nations sharing information about Antarctica, the Arctic, the oceans, the Earth's interior, and deep space.
- During IGY the 12 nations with scientific bases in Antarctica made maps and studied the weather, ice, and geology of the continent.

OVER, UNDER, AND THROUGH THE ICE

ON AUGUST 3, 1954, THE USS *NAUTILUS* BECAME the first submarine to reach the North Pole by navigating beneath the Arctic sea ice. Five Five years later the USS *Skate* went one better.

Using radar to pick a weak spot in the ice near the Pole, the submarine surfaced. The vessel punched a hole through the ice, and for the first time ever a submarine rested on the surface close to the North Pole. Surface ships soon followed. In 1977, the massive Russian icebreaker *Arktika* reached the North Pole, forcing her way through sea ice up to 13 ft (4 m) thick.

SUB MEETS BEAR
The Arctic is full of surprises. When the USS *Skate* surfaced at the Pole in 1959, the first thing the lookout saw was a polar bear!

IS IT A ROCKET?
Looking more like a spaceship than a submarine, the USS *Billfish* surfaces near the North Pole in 1987. The conning tower (the lookout containing the periscopes) juts through the ice with its fins pointing upward.

CHECKING THE FINS
The hydroplanes (control fins) on the sub's conning tower are vertical to break through the ice.

The ship's engineers check the fins for any damage.

THE BIG PICTURE
In polar regions, navigators receive satellite pictures by radio to help them find their way through the ice.

Radar scanners

Reinforced bow

Breaking the ice

ICEBREAKERS HAVE a specially shaped bow that allows them to ride up onto the ice. The ship's huge weight breaks through the ice to create a channel.

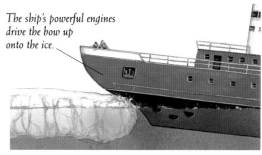

The ship's powerful engines drive the bow up onto the ice.

As the ice shatters, air pumped through holes in the hull pushes the fragments of ice away.

THE WAY THROUGH

The biggest icebreakers, like the Russian *Sovetskiy Soyuz* (above) can travel at a steady speed through ice up to 8 ft (2.4 m) thick, and can break through ice 23 ft (7 m) thick by backing up and ramming forward. Icebreakers often help Arctic and Antarctic research ships get through heavy pack ice.

HOLIDAY ON ICE

Tourists on a Russian icebreaker (left) wave to friends taking a helicopter ride as their ship pushes through heavy pack ice. Nearly 10,000 tourists visit Antarctica each year.

COOL SCIENCE

Marine biologists (scientists who study what lives in the sea) often have to dive far beneath the ice floes to see the fish, sea bed creatures, and seaweeds of the polar seas.

DOING IT THE HARD WAY

FOR SOME MEN AND WOMEN, IT'S not enough to make a long, exhausting, dangerous journey across a wilderness of snow and ice. For them, the challenge is to do it with as little help as possible. Some travel by dogsled in groups of two or three. Others walk to the North and South Poles entirely alone, pulling everything they need for survival on sleds weighing more than their own body weight. In 1993, two explorers achieved what many people thought was impossible – they hauled their own sleds across Antarctica.

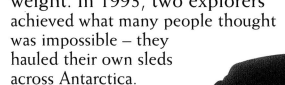

Following Shackleton
In 1994, Trevor Potts led a four-person British expedition that successfully sailed a replica of the *James Caird* (Shackleton's boat, see page 30) from Elephant Island to South Georgia in the South Atlantic.

EYEWITNESS

"Man has crossed the deserts and climbed the highest mountains...only one pioneer journey is left – a journey across the top of the world."

Wally Herbert in his book
Across the Top of the World, 1969

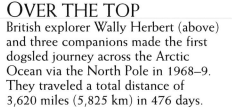

THE LONG WAY
In 1989–90, American Will Steger and Frenchman Jean-Louis Etienne (left) led an international team on a 4,000-mile (6,440-km) journey across Antarctica.

OVER THE TOP
British explorer Wally Herbert (above) and three companions made the first dogsled journey across the Arctic Ocean via the North Pole in 1968–9. They traveled a total distance of 3,620 miles (5,825 km) in 476 days.

Ranulph RF 240 Fiennes

Antarctica Unsupported 1992-3

Manhauling

Ranulph RF 216 Fiennes

Antarctica Unsupported 1992-3

© Mike Stroud and Ranulph Fiennes

RF 216

Keeping warm

MODERN POLAR CLOTHING is light and flexible so that the wearer can move around easily. Several layers, with air trapped between them, keep the body warm. The outer layer is windproof, but also "breathes" so the inner layers do not get damp from perspiration.

Snow goggles
Zipped jacket
Thermal vest, long-johns and inner gloves
Wool shirt
Windproof pants
Waterproof jacket, pants, and mittens with cuffs
Inner and outer boots

TRANS-ANTARCTIC SLOG
The first unsupported crossing of Antarctica, by Ranulph Fiennes and Mike Stroud (left) in 1992–3, took 97 days of endurance and willpower. As if hunger, frostbite, and blisters were not enough, crevasses (below) were a constant danger for the two men.

FIRST LADY
In 1994, Norwegian Liv Arnesen was the first woman to ski solo to the South Pole. She covered 745 miles (1,200 km) in 50 days, hauling a sled.

FACT file

• At the start of their trek across Antarctica, Ranulph Fiennes and Mike Stroud's sleds weighed 485 lb (220 kg) each.

• In 1996–7, Polish explorer Marek Kaminski was the first man to walk to both Poles in one calendar year.

MADE IT!
Norwegians Odd Harald Hauge, Cato Zahl Pedersen, and Lars Ebbesen celebrate at the South Pole after reaching the most southerly point on the globe, on skis, on December 29, 1994.

WORKING IN ANTARCTICA

ANTARCTICA HAS NO NATIVE PEOPLE. The only humans on the continent are 10,000 scientists and technicians who operate the research stations during the summer, and several thousand tourists who visit by ship to see the spectacular scenery and wildlife. The stations, such as the British Halley Station shown here, are self-contained communities. During the summer, field parties go out by plane, tractor, and motor toboggan to study the rocks and glaciers. Through the dark winter months, Antarctica is almost deserted. Fewer than 1,000 people remain on the bases.

SOUTH POLE STATION
The US's Amundsen–Scott Station at the South Pole is 9,186 ft (2,800 m) above sea level. It is ringed by the flags of the 26 Antarctic Treaty nations.

UNLOADING
The Halley Station receives its food, fuel, medical, and scientific supplies by ship once a year.

LONG HAUL
Boxes have to be hauled by tractor from the unloading point on the sea ice to the base 9 miles (15 km) inland.

Generators

PACE aerials

PACE PROJECT
The huge PACE radar array (series of radar aerials) allows scientists to study more than 1.16 million sq miles (three million square kilometers) of space above the South Pole.

Ice and Climate Building

A melt-tank uses waste heat from generators to melt snow for water.

ICE AND CLIMATE
A special building contains the ice, weather, and climate laboratories. Some scientists study the weather systems of the lower atmosphere; others use radar to study conditions more than 62 miles (100 km) above the Earth's surface.

ICE TUNNEL
During severe blizzards, scientists can reach the Ice and Climate Building, and other outlying buildings, through tunnels leading from the main block.

SOUTHERN LIGHTS

The *aurora australis* or "southern lights," visible in the Antarctic, are caused by charged particles from the sun hitting atoms of gas in the atmosphere. Similar "northern lights" are seen in the Arctic sky.

HALLEY STATION

The most modern of the British Antarctic Survey's five bases in Antarctica is named Halley. It specializes in atmospheric physics and climate studies.

Polar air lift

The US's Amundsen-Scott station at the South Pole is so remote that staff spending the winter are dependent on supplies flown in by Hercules C-130 airplanes.

No time to waste
Personnel work 24 hours a day to get supply planes unloaded and away before the weather changes.

MEDICAL RESEARCH
Doctors in Antarctica study how the human body reacts to cold, stress, long periods without daylight, and changes in diet.

Communications area

Tractor

GARAGE ON SKIS
The 60 ft (18 m), 55-ton (50-metric-ton) garage is mounted on skis. Each summer it is towed onto a snow mound so that its doors can swing open freely.

Kitchen and food storage

Leisure areas

Caterpillar tractor with snow shovel

Skidoo (motor toboggan)

Meteorological balloon

KEEPING FIT
A well-equipped gym helps off-duty personnel keep in shape, especially in winter when blizzards often prevent outside activity.

JACK-UP SYSTEM
Each building at Halley is on a steel platform held 13 ft (4 m) above the snow on mechanical jacks.

WEATHER BALLOON

Hydrogen-filled balloons, tracked by radar, allow scientists to study the winds above the Earth's surface.

LIVING QUARTERS

The accommodation building contains generator rooms, a communications center, the base office, computer room, dining room, kitchen, lounge, library, and 20 bunk rooms.

FACT file

- Eighteen countries operate Antarctic research stations.
- Under the Antarctic Treaty of 1961 the continent is reserved for science and must not be used for military or industrial purposes.
- The Treaty has strict environmental rules protecting Antarctic plant and animal life.

ALL ABOUT THE POLES

THE POLAR REGIONS are fascinating places for scientists. Physicists studying Earth's atmosphere from Antarctic research stations discovered the "hole" in the ozone layer. Geologists have found fossils showing how the continents have moved. Glaciologists have uncovered the story of the ice ages, and specialists learn more each year about global warming from sea ice, oceans, and glaciers.

An ice floe is a large flat piece of sea ice floating freely.

Brash ice is a jumbled mass of broken-up and half-melted fragments.

Ice terms
Glaciologists (scientists who study glaciers and icecaps) have special terms for ice formations. The photograph above shows some of the main ice features you would see on a typical stretch of Arctic coastline.

Rafting occurs when one ice floe is pushed up and slides on top of another.

A pressure ridge is a steep ridge of ice where two floes have been rammed together.

MOVING POLES
The Earth's magnetic field slowly changes, as if the imaginary magnet inside it is moving. As a result, the Magnetic Poles wander. James Clark Ross plotted the position of the South Magnetic Pole far inland. Today it is in the sea off the coast of Adelie Land.

MAGNETIC NORTH POLE IN 1831
MAGNETIC NORTH NOW

The drifter
Scientists have plotted the movement of the North Magnetic Pole for years. It is now near Ellef Ringnes Island, Canada, 870 miles (1,400 km) from the true North Pole.

ALBEDO
The "albedo" is the reflecting power of a surface. Soil and grass reflect only 10% of the sun's rays but snow and ice reflect 90%. That's why sunburn and snow blindness are dangers at the Poles.

Low glare
The land reflects 10% of the sun's rays, an albedo of 0.1.

High glare
Snow and ice reflect 90% of the sunlight, an albedo of 0.9.

Earth's magnetism
Earth is surrounded by an invisible magnetic field, just as if there was a large bar magnet inside it. The magnetism is caused by movements in the iron-rich molten rocks of the Earth's outer core. The magnetic force lines meet at the North and South Magnetic Poles.

A compass needle will always line itself up with the magnetic force lines, wherever you are on the globe.

At the North (and South) Magnetic Pole, compass needles point straight down!

South Magnetic Pole

Imaginary bar magnet

Timeline
The ribbon below represents the total time since the Earth was formed. We know very little about the first four billion years, but scientists have pieced together the story of the last few hundred million years using fossils and other clues locked in the Earth's rocks.

Icebergs represent ice ages, volcanoes represent major geological events, and figures represent the arrival of humans.

Great Southern Ice Age begins

Breakup of supercontinent. Plants and dinosaurs on Antarctic continent

Volcanic activity as continents drift apart

Antarctic glaciers form

Last Ice Age begins

This section of the timeline represents the last 2 million years >

| 300 MILLION YEARS AGO | 200MYA | 100MYA | 300,000 YEARS AGO |

345 MILLION YEARS AGO (MYA) 200MYA 150MYA 30MYA 2MYA

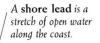

A **shore lead** *is a stretch of open water along the coast.*

Fast ice *is thick, old ice that is stuck fast to the rocks along the shore.*

A **frozen lead** *is a patch of previously open water that has frozen over with clear blue ice.*

Icebergs are are shaped by waves and by melting under the sun.

"BATWING" ICEBERG

THE BIG BREAKUP

In the past, Earth's land areas have broken apart, then drifted to their present positions. The last big breakup started 200 million years ago when Antarctica, Australia, Africa, and South America split and separated.

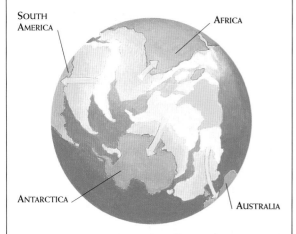

SOUTH AMERICA

AFRICA

ANTARCTICA

AUSTRALIA

Fossil clues
Fossil ferns in Antarctic rocks show that the continent was not always so cold. In the past it was closer to the equator.

ANTARCTIC FOSSIL FERN

Polar summer and winter

BECAUSE THE EARTH'S axis is tilted, the amount of sunlight reaching the surface varies throughout the year. When the North Pole is tilted toward the sun, it is summer north of the equator. Six months later the Earth has done half its yearly journey around the sun, the North Pole is tilted away, and it is winter in the north and summer in the south.

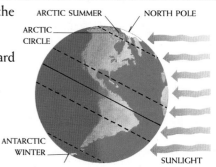

ARCTIC SUMMER

NORTH POLE

ARCTIC CIRCLE

ANTARCTIC WINTER

SUNLIGHT

Land of the midnight sun
At the Arctic Circle there are a few days each year when the sun never sets. It dips close to the horizon then rises back into the sky.

Northern summer, southern winter
At the North Pole, the sun stays above the horizon for the entire six months of Arctic summer. At the same time, the South Pole has six months of darkness.

TIME-LAPSE PHOTOGRAPH OF SUN'S POSITION OVER 24 HOURS

Ice cores
As each year's snow gets buried by the next, it turns to ice. The ice traps tiny air bubbles that preserve a sample of the atmosphere at the time the snow fell. The ice layers also contain dust from volcanoes, and insects and pollen blown by the wind. Scientists drill ice cores in order to study these clues to the past. The deepest ice cores, near the Russian 'Vostock Research Station in Antarctica, reach 11,886 ft (3,623 m) in depth and contain ice that is 400,000 years old.

LIFTING OUT THE ICE CORE

WATER FREEZING IN THE AIR

FROZEN MAGIC
At very low air temperatures, a cup of boiling water thrown into the air will explode in a shower of hissing vapor trails and ice crystals. (Don't try this. It works only in extreme climates and you could scald yourself.)

FROZEN FACE

Ice mask
In polar regions, the water vapor in a person's breath turns to ice on the face, freezing beards and moustaches.

Glaciation period

Glaciation period

Last ice age ends. Humans settle in the Arctic

200,000YA

100,000YA

125,000YA

45,000YA

10,000YA

WHO WENT WHERE AND WHEN?

The entries below describe some of the world's great polar explorers and their remarkable achievements.

ARCTIC EXPLORERS

1553
Hugh Willoughby (UK)
Led the first British attempt to find a Northeast Passage, but died trying to winter on the Kola Peninsula.

1576–8
Martin Frobisher (UK)
English navigator who made three voyages in search of a Northwest Passage (see page 8).

1585–7
John Davis (UK)
The Davis Strait between Greenland and Baffin Island is named after him. He also discovered the Falkland Islands in 1592 (see page 8).

VOYAGE TO THE ARCTIC

1594–7
William Barents (Neth.)
Made three voyages in search of a Northwest Passage (see page 9).

1607–11
Henry Hudson (UK)
Attempted to find the Northeast and Northwest Passages (see page 8).

AN ESKIMO HUNTING SEAL

1616
William Baffin (UK)
Sailed farther into the Arctic than anyone before him. Discovered Baffin Bay, Ellesmere Island, and Baffin Island.

1648
Semyon Dezhnev (Russia)
First to sail through the channel between Russia and Alaska. Reports of his discovery were lost so the channel was named after Bering, the next man to sail through it.

1725–30
Vitus Bering (Den.)
Discovered Alaska and explored the coast of Siberia (see page 9).

1818
John Ross (UK)
While searching for the Northwest Passage, he sailed into Lancaster Sound but turned back, convinced it was a dead end. Later explorers found a way through.

1819–20
William Parry (UK)
Discovered part of the Northwest Passage (page 9). On a later expedition he tried to get to the North Pole across the ice and reached 82°45′N.

1819–22
John Franklin (UK)
Explored the Canadian Arctic, including coast that later formed part of the Northwest Passage (see page 8).

CROSSING LAKE PROSPEROUS

1820–23
Ferdinand von Wrangel (Russia)
Explored the coast of Siberia by dogsled and discovered an island now named after him.

1831
James Clark Ross (UK)
Discovered the position of the North Magnetic Pole (see also page 47).

AT THE NORTH MAGNETIC POLE

1845–7
John Franklin (UK)
His last fateful journey was in the ships *Erebus* and *Terror* (see The Lost Expedition, pages 14-15).

1875–6
George Nares (UK)
Traveled through the Arctic pack ice as far as latitude 83°20′N.

1878–80
Adolf Nordenskjold (Sweden)
The first to navigate a ship through the Northeast Passage from west to east.

1879–81
George De Long (US)
Proved that Arctic sea ice is moved by ocean currents. His ship *Jeannette* drifted 310 miles (500 km) in 21 months.

1888–96
Fridtjof Nansen (Norway)
Made the first crossing of the Greenland icecap on skis. See also The Voyage of the *Fram*, pages 16-17.

1897
Salomon Andrée (Sweden)
See Three Men in a Balloon, pages 18-19.

1899–1900
Luigi Amedeo (Italy)
Led the first Italian expedition to winter in the Arctic.

1903–1906
Roald Amundsen (Nor.)
The first to sail through the Northwest Passage, in his ship *Gjoa*.

1905–1909
Robert Peary (US)
See On Top of the World, pages 22-23.

1913–15
Vilkitski (Russia)
Made the first east-to-west voyage through the Northeast Passage.

1926
Roald Amundsen (Nor.), Lincoln Ellsworth (US), Umberto Nobile (Italy)
Made the first flight over the North Pole in an airship (see page 33).

1928
Umberto Nobile (Italy)
Reached the North Pole in the airship *Italia*, but crashed on return flight.

1937–8
Ivan Papanin (Russia)
Set up the first drifting polar observatory at the North Pole.

AN ESKIMO WITH DOGS

1968
Ralph Plaisted (US)
First to reach the North Pole using skidoos (motorized toboggans).

1968–9
Wally Herbert (UK)
Led the first Trans-Arctic Expedition. See page 40.

1978
Naome Uemura (Japan)
Made the first solo journey to the North Pole with a dogsled.

1988–92
Helen Thayer (NZ)
First woman to make a solo journey to the North Magnetic Pole. She and her husband Bill were the oldest couple (54 and 65) to reach it on foot in 1992.

Explorer's timeline
On the timeline below, the figures on skis represent the first landings in polar regions and journeys made over land or sea ice. The plane symbol represents flights made by balloon, airship, and airplane.

PARRY 1819–20   WILKES 1838   D'URVILLE 1837   JAMES CLARK ROSS 1842   ANDRÉE 1897

| 1810 | 1820 | 1830 | 1840 | 1850 | 1860 | 1870 | 1880 | 1890 | 190 |

JOHN ROSS 1818   FRANKLIN 1846   NANSEN 1895

ANTARCTIC EXPLORERS

1773
James Cook (UK)
Crossed the Antarctic Circle with two ships, *Resolution* and *Adventure* (see page 11).

A PENGUIN GETS TOO CLOSE

1819–21
Fabian von Bellingshausen (Russia)
Sailed around Antarctica (see page 10).

1820
Edward Bransfield (UK)
Mapped part of the north coast of the Antarctic Peninsula.

1820
Nathaniel Palmer (US)
Discovered part of the Antarctic Peninsula and later (1821–2) the South Orkney Islands.

1823
James Weddell (UK)
Reached latitude 74°15′S with the *Jane* and the *Beaufroy* in what was later named the Weddell Sea in his honor.

1830–32
John Biscoe (UK)
One of several sealers and whalers who made Antarctic discoveries. He discovered parts of the Antarctic Peninsula (Graham Land and Adelaide Island).

SLEDDING IN THE ANTARCTIC

1837–40
Dumont d'Urville (Fr.)
Mapped part of the north Graham Land coast and its offshore islands, and Adelie Land (see page 11).

1838–42
Charles Wilkes (US)
Discovered and mapped a long section of the Antarctic coast (see page 10).

1839–43
James Clark Ross (UK)
Located the position of the South Magnetic Pole and made many important discoveries in the Antarctic (see South Through the Ross Sea, pages 12–13).

A SOCCER MATCH ON ICE

1898–1900
Carsten Borchgrevink (Norway)
One of the first to land on the Antarctic mainland, in 1895. In 1898 he returned as leader of the British Southern Cross Expedition.

1901–4
Robert Falcon Scott (UK)
Spent the winter onboard the *Discovery*, in McMurdo Sound.

1903–5
Jean-Baptiste Charcot (France)
Mapped the west coast of the Antarctic Peninsula, then returned in 1908–10 to look for a sea route to the South Pole. Drowned in 1936 when his ship sank on an expedition to Greenland.

1907–9
Ernest Shackleton (UK)
In an attempt to reach the South Pole, his party got to within 100 miles (160 km) of the Pole.

1910–12
Roald Amundsen (Nor.)
See Race to the South Pole, pages 24–25.

1910–12
Robert Falcon Scott (UK)
See Race to the South Pole, pages 24–25

1911–12
Wilhelm Filchner (Germany)
Discovered and named the Filchner Ice Shelf in the Weddell Sea.

1911–14
Douglas Mawson (Aus.)
Accompanied Shackleton on the 1907–9 expedition. Returned as leader of an Australian expedition, 1911–14 (see The Loneliest March, pages 26–27).

1914–16
Ernest Shackleton (UK)
See The Great Escape, pages 28-31.

1921–2
Ernest Shackleton (UK)
His last expedition – to sail around Antarctica in the *Quest* – was cut short when he died on board the ship.

1928–30
Hubert Wilkins (Aus.)
Australian pilot who made the first flights in Antarctica.

USING A SAIL TO HELP PULL A SLED

1928–34
Richard Byrd (US)
Flew over vast areas of Antarctica. In 1929 he made the first flight over the South Pole, flying there and back from the base "Little America." See also pages 32-33.

1935–6
Lincoln Ellsworth (US)
Made the first flight across Antarctica, in a Northrop monoplane (see page 33).

EXERCISING A PONY

1946–7
Operation Highjump
Under the command of Richard Byrd and Admiral Cruzen, 4,000 US servicemen began mapping Antarctica using aerial photography.

1957–8
Vivian Fuchs (UK) and Edmund Hillary (NZ)
Led the Commonwealth Trans-Antarctic Expedition. See A Continent for Science, pages 36-37.

1968–9
A Japanese expedition traveled to the South Pole from the Japanese Syowa base on the coast of Enderby Land – a journey of over 3,373 miles (6,000 km).

1979–82
Ranulph Fiennes and Charles Burton (UK)
Completed the first (and only) nonstop journey around the globe, crossing over both the North Pole and the South Pole.

1985–6
"In the Footsteps of Scott" expedition
Roger Swan, Roger Mear, and Gareth Wood set out to retrace Scott's journey to the South Pole. They reached the American Amundsen–Scott base at the Pole on January 11, 1986.

1989–90
Will Steger (US), Jean-Louis Etienne (France)
Led a six-man expedition down the Antarctic Peninsula and across the widest part of the continent – a distance of 4,008 miles (6,450 km).

1992–3
Erling Kagge (Norway)
Manhauled, solo, to the South Pole without air or land support.

AT THE SOUTH POLE

1992–93
Ranulph Fiennes and Mike Stroud (UK)
The first unsupported crossing of Antarctica, manhauling a distance of 1,350 miles (2,173 km).

1994
Liv Arnesen (Norway)
The first woman to ski solo to the South Pole.

1995–6
Marek Kaminski (Pol.)
Reached the North and South Poles in one year.

PEARY 1905–9
AMUNDSEN 1911
SCOTT 1912
MAWSON 1913

AMUNDSEN, ELLSWORTH, AND NOBILE 1926

FUCHS/HILLARY 1957–8

WALLY HERBERT 1968–9

FIENNES/BURTON 1979–82

FIENNES/STROUD 1992–3
ETIENNE/STEGER 1989

KAMINSKI 1996
ARNESEN 1994
KAGGE 1993

BYRD 1926–9

THAYER 1988

| 1920 | 1930 | 1940 | 1950 | 1960 | 1970 | 1980 | 1990 |

SHACKLETON 1914–16

ELLSWORTH 1935

UEMURA 1978

Index

Acknowledgments

The publisher would like to thank: Robert Graham for research, Chris Bernstein for the index, Venice Shone and Peter Radcliffe for design help, Philippa Smith at Scott Polar Research Institute, and British Antarctic Survey.

The publisher would like to thank the following for their kind permission to reproduce their photographs:

c=center; t=top; b=bottom; l=left; r=right; a=above

AKG, London: 33cra/br; Brian and Cherry Alexander Photography: 17cr, 39c, 44/45t; Ann Hawthorne 12bl, 41cra/bc, 42tr, 43tr; Hans Reinhard 11cla; Archive Photos: 38cla; Barnaby's Picture Library: PMR Rothman 45cra; British Antarctic Survey: C.J.Gilbert 45bl; B.Herrod 45cr (below); Ash Johnson 37tr; A.King 43tl; Robert Mulvaney 45bc; J.Pickup 45cr; The Beinecke Rare Book & Manuscript Library/Yale University: 10cl (below); The Bridgeman Art Library: British Library: 9bl; British Museum: John White 8bc; National Maritime Museum: John Harrison 11tc; Royal Geographical Society: Critical Position of H.M.S Investigator on the North Coast of Baring Island, Lieu.S.Gurney Cresswell (published 1854) 6/7b; Christie's Images: 15tr; Bruce Coleman: Mr Johnny Johnson 10c; Corbis: 11bc, 22tl, 33cl (below); Mary Evans Picture Library: 23br; ET Archive: 8cl, 11tr; Robert Harding Picture Library: National Maritime Museum 11cr; Motoway 40c; Hedgehog House, New Zealand: Tim Higham 34/35c; Colin Monteath 24cla, 39tl, 40tl, 45cla; Hulton Getty Images: 20/21b, 32tl; Katz Pictures Limited: Mansell/Time Inc. 27br; The Mawson Antarctic Collection/The University of Adelaide: 26bc, 27tr/bl/bc; Mittet Foto: 16bl, 32bl, 33tr; National Maritime Museum: 23tc, 25clb; Planet Earth Pictures: B & C Alexander 23tr; Jonathan Scott 10bc; The Royal Botanic Gardens, Kew: 11br; The Royal Geographical Society Picture Library: 9cb, 14br, 36bl, 37bc; Ranulph Fiennes 41cla/tl/c; Martha Holmes 9cla; Scott Polar Research Institute: 19cra/crb/br, 25br, 28tl, 30tl, 31br; Sygma: 40bl; Stephana Compoint 39br; Topham Picturepoint: 9cra; TRH Pictures: US Navy 38b; University of Alberta / Department of Anthropology: Owen Beattie 14bc; University of Oslo Library Picture Department: 17br

Jacket: National Maritime Museum: front cover c/cl (below)/bl, inside front tl, inside back tr

Every effort has been made to trace the copyright holders of written material and we apologise for any ommisions. We would be pleased to insert an appropriate acknowledgement in any subsequent edition of this publication.

Roald Amundsen, My Life as an explorer (William Heinemann, London, 1927); Sir Vivian Fuchs, The Crossing of Antarctica, (Cassell, London, 1958); Wally Herbert, Across the Top of the World, ©Wally Herbert (Penguin, 1969); Sir Douglas Mawson, The Home of the Blizzard (William Heinemann, London, 1915); Robert Peary, The North Pole (London, 1910); Robert F. Scott, final diaries and letters (SPRI) /Scott's Last Expedition (London, 1913); Ernest Shackleton, South (William Heinemann, London, 1919).